D1611588

Machines and Motion

# Inclined Planes

by Kirsten Chang

Bullfrog
Books

# Ideas for Parents and Teachers

Bullfrog Books let children practice reading informational text at the earliest reading levels. Repetition, familiar words, and photo labels support early readers.

## Before Reading
- Discuss the cover photo. What does it tell them?
- Look at the picture glossary together. Read and discuss the words.

## Read the Book
- "Walk" through the book and look at the photos. Let the child ask questions. Point out the photo labels.
- Read the book to the child, or have him or her read independently.

## After Reading
- Prompt the child to think more. Ask: Inclined planes are everywhere. Where do you see them? What do they help you accomplish?

Bullfrog Books are published by Jump!
5357 Penn Avenue South
Minneapolis, MN 55419
www.jumplibrary.com

Library of Congress Cataloging-in-Publication Data

Names: Chang, Kirsten, author.
Title: Inclined planes / by Kirsten Chang.
Description: Minneapolis, MN : Jump!, Inc., [2018]
Series: Machines and motion
Audience: Ages 5–8. | Audience: K to grade 3.
Includes bibliographical references and index.
Identifiers: LCCN 2017052358 (print)
LCCN 2017051350 (ebook)
ISBN 9781624968501 (ebook)
ISBN 9781624968488 (hardcover : alk. paper)
ISBN 9781624968495 (pbk.)
Subjects: LCSH: Inclined planes—Juvenile literature.
Simple machines—Juvenile literature.
Classification: LCC TJ147 (print)
LCC TJ147 .C4535 2018 (ebook) | DDC 621.8/11—dc23
LC record available at https://lccn.loc.gov/2017052358

Editor: Kristine Spanier
Book Designer: Molly Ballanger

Photo Credits: SabOlga/Shutterstock, cover; Jessi et Nono/Shutterstock, 1; Kittisak Hanpol/Shutterstock, 3; ESB Professional/Shutterstock, 4, 8; Local Favorite Photography/Shutterstock, 5, 23tr; max blain/ Shutterstock, 6–7; Zen Sekizawa/Getty, 9, 23bl; Oleg Totskyi/Shutterstock, 10–11, 23br; katueng/ Shutterstock, 12–13, 23tl; Wavebreakmedia/iStock, 14; Bill45/Shutterstock, 15; Kritsana/Shutterstock, 16–17; Brocreative/Shutterstock, 18–19; Andriy Blokhin/ Shutterstock, 20–21; Mike Flippo/Shutterstock, 24.

Printed in the United States of America at Corporate Graphics in North Mankato, Minnesota.

# Table of Contents

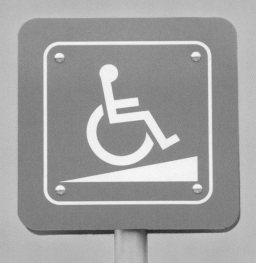

# Up and Down

What is an
inclined plane?

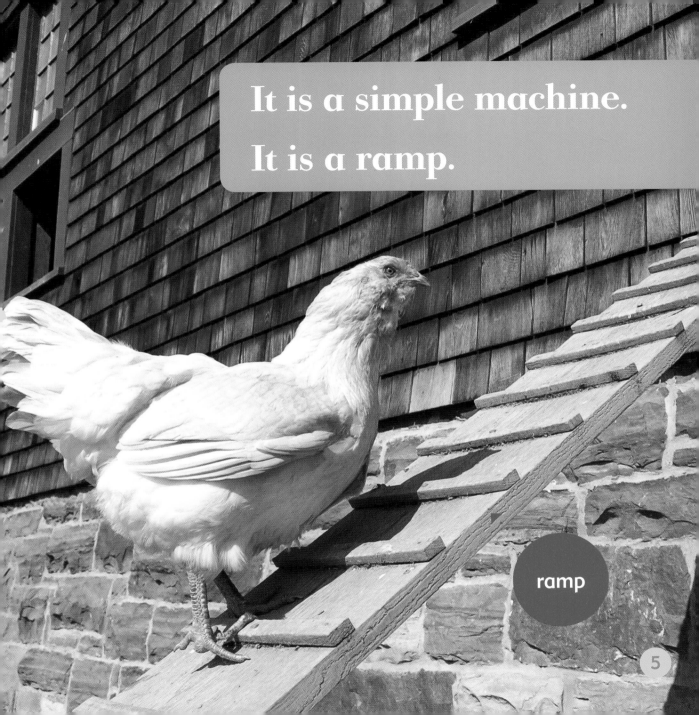

It is a simple machine.

It is a ramp.

ramp

5

One end is higher than the other.

This makes it easy to move things up and down.

**Ty carries a box.**

How will he get
it in the truck?

He uses a ramp.

9

All aboard!
A trolley travels
up a ramp.

10

trolley

belt

See the moving belt?
It is a ramp.
It lifts our bags.

Ray uses a wheelchair.
How does he get
to the door?

A ramp!

ramp

Ramps can be fun.
Rides take us high.
Ramps get us there.

A slide is a ramp.
Whee!

# How do you use inclined planes?

# Build an Inclined Plane

**Build your own inclined plane to test out how things slide or roll down.**

## You will need:

- large piece of cardboard
- blocks or stack of books
- objects to send down your ramp:
  - balls
  - crayons
  - toy cars
  - spoon
  - book

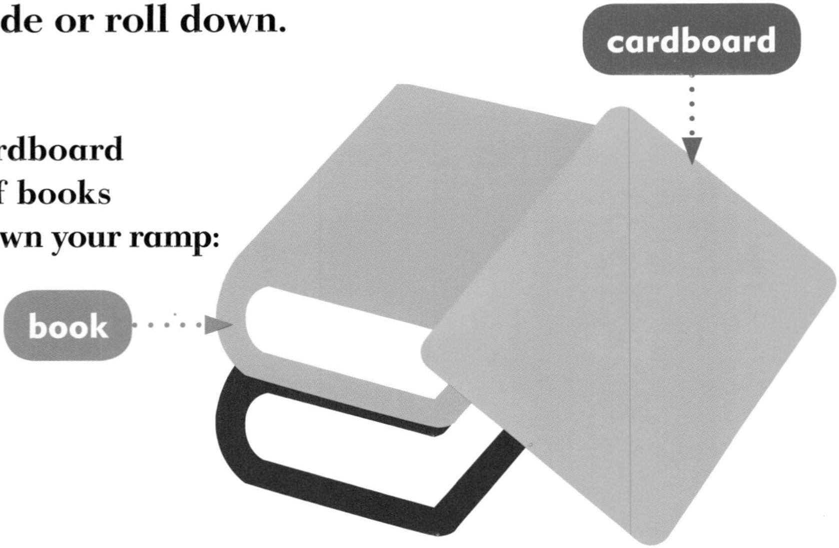

cardboard

book

## Directions:

❶ Make a ramp by propping the piece of cardboard on a stack of blocks or books.

❷ Gather some objects to send down your ramp. Guess what will happen to each object before you push it down the ramp. Will it roll? Will it slide? Will it stay in place?

❸ Change the height of your ramp by adding or taking away the blocks or books under it. What happens to each object now?

# Picture Glossary

**belt**
A continuous moving band that moves objects from one place to another.

**simple machine**
A tool used to make work easier, such as an inclined plane, lever, pulley, screw, wedge, or wheel and axle.

**inclined plane**
A flat surface that makes an angle with the line of the horizon.

**trolley**
A car that runs on tracks and carries people.

# Index

# To Learn More

Learning more is as easy as 1, 2, 3.

1) Go to www.factsurfer.com

2) Enter "inclinedplanes" into the search box.

3) Click the "Surf" button to see a list of websites.

With factsurfer.com, finding more information is just a click away.